T0193276

I Have a Savior

Written and illustrated by
Isabella Theodora

WestBow Press books may be ordered through booksellers or by contacting:

WestBow Press
A Division of Thomas Nelson & Zondervan
1663 Liberty Drive
Bloomington, IN 47403
www.westbowpress.com
844-714-3454

Because of the dynamic nature of the Internet, any web addresses or links contained in this book may have changed since publication and may no longer be valid. The views expressed in this work are solely those of the author and do not necessarily reflect the views of the publisher, and the publisher hereby disclaims any responsibility for them.

Any people depicted in stock imagery provided by Getty Images are models, and such images are being used for illustrative purposes only. Certain stock imagery © Getty Images.

Scripture quotations are from the ESV Bible® (The Holy Bible, English Standard Version®), copyright © 2001 by Crossway Bibles, a publishing ministry of Good News Publishers. Used by permission. All rights reserved.

ISBN: 979-8-3850-0923-7 (sc)
ISBN: 979-8-3850-0925-1 (hc)
ISBN: 979-8-3850-0924-4 (e)

Library of Congress Control Number: 2023918972

Print information available on the last page.

WestBow Press rev. date: 10/13/2023

WESTBOW
PRESS®
A DIVISION OF THOMAS NELSON
& ZONDERVAN

Dedication:

For Holy Spirit,
My leader, my guide, my counselor, my helper, my comforter, my best friend, and my forever co-writer.

I will continue to exalt Him with my Life.

Acknowledgements:

I wanted to acknowledge the 3 most important people in my life at this time:

Pastor Sam King Flame,
Thank you for truly teaching me who Holy Spirit is and making me fall even more madly in love with Him as my helper and healer. Thank you for standing powerfully with our family in prayer and in the Word of God. This book is very greatly inspired by you.

To my Grandmother, Mary Wills,
You have always been one of the people I look up to the most and I treasure you. Thank you for teaching me who the Lord is and helping me draw nearer to Him each day.

And to my sister, Naomi Elizabeth,
I Love you dearly and I am so, so thankful for you in my life. Thank you for being my role model and best friend throughout my whole childhood, and most of all, thank you for Loving Jesus unconditionally and showing me how to live for Him and Love Him too.

I have a Savior
I have a friend
Who hears my heart, and
Each word I've said.

Yes, He loves me so,
Fully I know;
He will stand with me
Through sun and snow.

He speaks into me
With Fire and Light,

3

And sings me a song
Whispering bright,

Gleaming like lightning
Flashed from the dark,
Rolling like thunder,
Soft as a lark.

Power and wonder
Ring from His Face

Yet there is peace in
His gentle gaze

Peace like a river,
Might like the sea

Joy springing up in
Fountains of glee

Great in His power
Strong in His Word
Gleaming with beauty
My loving Lord

Voice filled with mercy,
power, and love,

Strong as a lion,
Kind as a dove.

He sings over me
Comforting me

Holding me closely
Carrying me.

Even through darkness,
Even through pain
He will stand with me,
Staying the same.

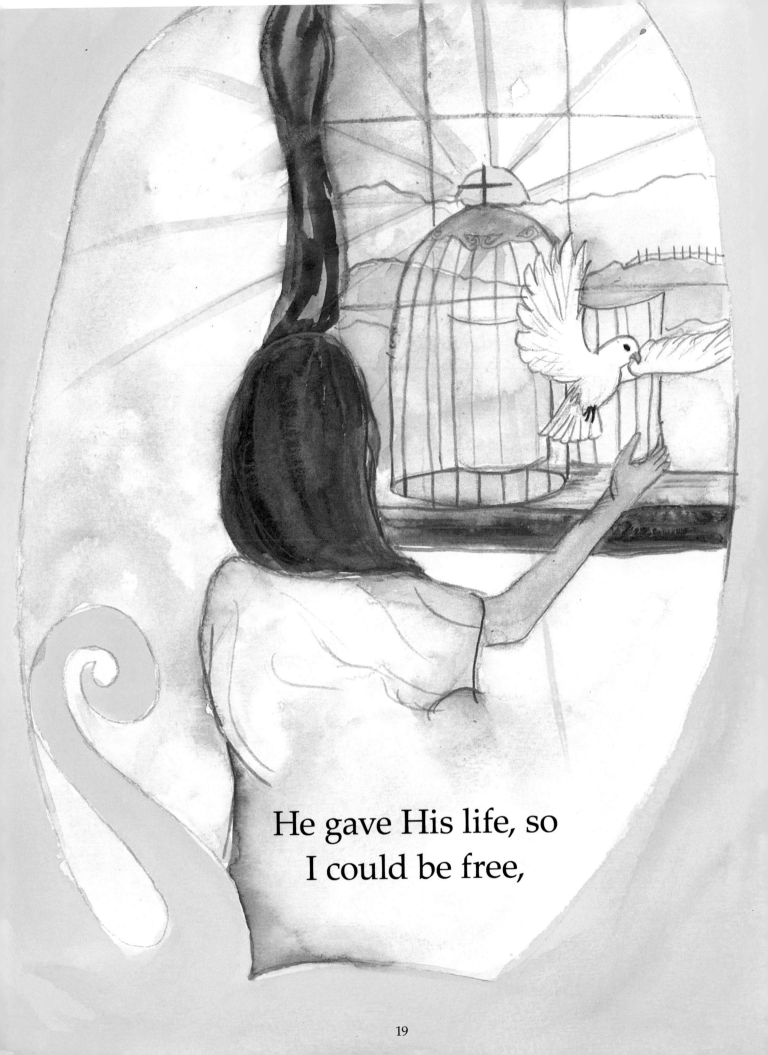

He gave His life, so
I could be free,

Free to come near Him,
Come, and to see

Free to be one with
Father above,
Gates thrown wide open
Through His great Love.

A child of God, now
Able to stand,
Fully to walk in
The promised land.

I've tasted and seen
His goodness to me
Refreshing to me
Like mist by the sea.

And all of my life,

And all that I am,

And all that I have,

Rests in His hand.

I have a Savior,
I have a friend,
Who hears my heart, and
Each word I've said

He Loves me so, and,
Fully I know,

He will stand with me,
Through sun and snow.

Printed in the United States
by Baker & Taylor Publisher Services